Introduction and Variation

THE CARNIVAL OF V
(op. posth.)

J. DEMERSSEMAN (1833-1866)
Arranged and edited by F. L. HEMKE.

ST-520

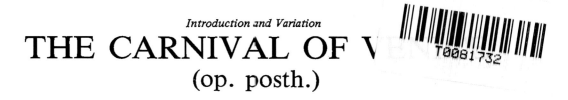

2

ST-520

4

ST-520

6

70 2nd Variation

Introduction and Variations on

Le Carnaval de Venise

by

Jules Demersseman

for

Alto Saxophone and Piano

edited by

Frederick Hemke

ALTO SAXCPHONE

Southern
MUSIC

Introduction and Variations

THE CARNIVAL OF VENICE
(op. posth.)

Eb Alto Saxophone

J. DEMERSSEMAN (1833-1866)
Arranged and edited by F. L. HEMKE.

Eb Alto Saxophone

2nd Variation

3rd Variation

Eb Alto Saxophone

110 **Finale** - This Variation to be played as fast as possible.

ABOUT THE WRITERS

Jules Auguste Edouard Demersseman (1833-1866) was a flutist and composer of outstanding qualities. Born in Holland, he spent most of his life in Paris, where he studied with the eminent Jean Louis Tulou. He was said to be endowed with lungs of impressive power and capacity, as well as fingers and tongue of incredible velocity. He dazzled audiences with lengthy cadenzas and pyrotechnics of his own writing, causing them to stand and shout with enthusiasm.

The Carnival of Venice was written for Adolphe Mayeur, a music director of the Imperial Guard Band and an accomplished saxophone performer. Mayeur had actually been one of Adolphe Sax's students and was also a friend of Demersseman. The *Carnival,* published posthumously in 1867, was first printed by the "House of Adolphe Sax, Patented Manufacturer of the Emperor's Military."

Frederick L. Hemke (b. July 11, 1935) is a world renowned saxophonist. In 1956, he became the first American to be awarded the prestigious Premiere Prix de Saxophone at Conservatoire National Supérieur de Musique, Paris, where he was a student of Marcel Mule. In 1975, Dr. Hemke published *The Early History of the Saxophone*, a mammoth dissertation which explored in depth the saxophone's history and gradual acceptance in the realm of symphonic music. An active recitalist and performer with orchestras and wind ensembles worldwide, he has made recordings with the Chicago Symphony Orchestra, Kronos Quartet, Stockholm Philharmonic, Eastman Wind Ensemble, and Contemporary Chamber Players as well as solo albums. Widely regarded by his peers as a master player and educator, Dr. Hemke is also a legendary reedmaker, and a well known brand name of reeds for woodwind instruments bears Hemke's name. For many years Dr. Hemke has been Professor of Music at Northwestern University in Evanston, Illinois. His students teach and perform in major teaching and performing positions throughout the world.

* * * * *

The Carnival of Venice is available for performance with concert band. The accompaniment, written in traditional "concert-in-the-park" style, is by Herbert L. Clarke and Mark Rogers. The score and parts are available on a rental basis from Southern Music Company. Please telephone (210) 226-8167 or fax (210) 223-4537 or e-mail info@southernmusic.com for further information.

8

86 3rd Variation

10

This Variation to be played fast as possible

125 Coda-più presto